DATE DUE

JAN 0 7 2003	
MAR 1 6 2003	
3 92 25	

THREE POETS OF MODERN KOREA

♦

THREE POETS OF MODERN KOREA

*Yi Sang, Hahm Dong-seon
and Choi Young-mi*

Translated by
Yu Jung-yul
and James Kimbrell

Sarabande  Books
LOUISVILLE, KENTUCKY

Copyright © 2002 by Yu Jung-yul and James Kimbrell

No part of this book may be reproduced without written permission of the publisher. Please direct inquiries to:

Managing Editor
Sarabande Books, Inc.
2234 Dundee Road, Suite 200
Louisville, KY 40205

LIBRARY OF CONGRESS CATALOGING-IN-PUBLICATION DATA

Yi, Sang, 1910–1937.
Three poets of modern Korea : Yi Sang, Hahm Dong-seon, and Choi
Young-mi / translated and edited by Yu Jung-yul and James Kimbrell.
p.   cm.
ISBN 1-889330-71-X (alk. paper)
1. Yi, Sang, 1910-1937—Translations into English. 2. Hahm, Dong-seon—
Translations into English. 3. Choi, Young-mi, 1961—Translations into
English. I. Title: 3 poets of modern Korea. II. Hahm, Dong-seon. III. Choi,
Young-mi, 1961– IV. Yu, Jung-yul, 1969–
V. Kimbrell, James, 1967– VI. Title.

PL991.9.S3 A29 2002
895.7'1408—dc21   2001049529

Cover image: *Paik Nam-june Performing Violin To Be Dragged on the Street* by
Peter Moore. Photograph by Peter Moore © Est. Peter Moore/VAGA, NYC.

Cover and text design by Charles Casey Martin
Photograph of Choi Young-mi (page 49) by Chung Yeon-shim
Photograph of James Kimbrell (page 81) by Jennifer Eriksen

Manufactured in the United States of America
This book is printed on acid-free paper.

Sarabande Books is a nonprofit literary organization.

Funded in part by a grant from the Kentucky Arts Council, a state agency of
the Education, Arts, and Humanities Cabinet

FIRST EDITION

This book is dedicated to our parents.

CONTENTS

♦

Hahm Dong-seon

Choi Young-mi

ACKNOWLEDGMENTS

◆

We would like to thank editors of the following magazines in which these translations first appeared, sometimes in slightly different form: *Chattahoochee Review:* "In Tunnel Number Three," "Autumn Sanjo," "Journal in Jumunjin," "In the Season of Ripened Barley...," "The Last Face." *Fence:* "Crow's-Eye View, Poem No. V," "Crow's-Eye View, Poem No. XIII." *Field:* "I Wed a Toy Bride," "Crow's-Eye View, Poem No. X: Butterfly," "Crow's-Eye View, Poem No. XV." *Mississippi Review (World Poetry 2000):* "A Rough Sketch of Autumn," "Fisherman's Morning," "For T____, Light Red over Black," "Birds, Even Now...." *Pleiades:* "Dead Leaf and Child." *Poetry:* "Record of a Journey," "Jeju Island." *Salt Fork Review:* "Island," "Full Moon," "Thought in Several Pieces." *Third Coast:* "In a Subway, #4," "In Sokcho," In the Submerged Area of Imha Dam," "A Page from My Childhood Journal."

◆

Poems translated here are from the following books published in the Korean:

Yi Sang

Collected Works of Yi Sang, I. Yi Seung-hun (ed.). Seoul: Munhak Sasang Sa, 1989.

Hahm Dong-seon

    Short Time, Long Story. Seoul: Sanmok, 1997.

    Thinking of Home from a Distance. Seoul: Kyongwon Publishers,
      1994.

    Colony. Seoul: Chunghan Munhwa Sa, 1986.

Choi Young-mi

    At Thirty, the Party Was Over. Seoul: Changbi, 1994.

    Bicycling in Dreamland. Seoul: Changbi, 1998.

◆

We would like to thank the Mrs. Giles Whiting Foundation for their encouragement and financial support. We are grateful as well to Florida State University for the funding and release time that helped greatly in the completion of this manuscript. We are especially grateful to Hahm Dong-seon and Choi Young-mi for their friendship, for their poems, and for their editorial willingness and insight. Thanks as well to Angela Ball and Lee Hye-won for their indispensable editorial suggestions. Our sincere appreciation to Sarah Gorham for her vision and untiring support.

INTRODUCTION

♦

Pusan, South Korea. The D.J. on the taxi's radio shouts, "Yi Sang is the greatest poet of the twentieth century!" Apparently, we are tuned in to a show dedicated to pop songs derived from transpositions of Korean poems ranging from modern to ancient, demotic to hermetic, celebratory to elegiac. This should come as no surprise in a country where poems are found on mountain boulders, on café walls, on placemats, T-shirts, and television game shows, a country in which every candidate for civil service had to pass an exam establishing proficiency as a poet, a one thousand-year-old requirement relaxed only in the past one hundred years.

And yet, the story of Korea in the twentieth century is a story in which language itself has been counted as a criminal, if not capital, offense. Ruled by Japan for much of the first half of the twentieth century, Korean people were given Japanese names, forced to adopt Japanese customs, and lived for much of this time under a law that prohibited Korean newspapers, magazines, patriotic songs, and public assembly. When colonization ended with Hirohito's surrender to the Allies in 1945, Japan agreed to withdraw from Korea. The withdrawal, however, was to be supervised by the Soviet Union north of the 38th parallel and by the United States in the South, a division aggravated by domestic and international tensions that led to the three-year period of bloodshed, starvation, rape, and exile known as the Korean War.

The division now goes by the name of the DMZ, a heavily patrolled demilitarized zone a mile-and-a-half wide and one hundred and fifty miles long that separates the Korean people even today. In the South, this physical boundary has too often found its correlative in military regimes quick to repress writers thought to have sympathies with the North. As for the North, the gates of poetry are shut airtight; we have little, if any, idea of what literary activity outside the auspices of propaganda might be (and surely must be) transpiring there.

♦

"Yi Sang is the greatest poet of the twentieth century!" We'll leave that claim to the arbiters of cultural value and canonicity. There is little doubt, however, that he is an innovative, energetic, enigmatic, and sometimes absolutely bewildering poet. When an installment of his "Crow's-Eye View" appeared in the pages of the *Chosun Chungang Ilbo* in 1934, the newspaper received so many complaints that it declined to print the remaining installments. Yi Sang's work had managed to purposefully and generously transgress the comparatively staunch decorum of the poetry to which his first readers were accustomed. But his was a literary milieu inflected by dada and surrealism that came to Korea primarily (and ironically) via the Japanese imperialists and from their rivals in the pursuit of Pacific domain, the French. Yi Sang (born Kim Hae-gyeong in Seoul, 1910) was trained as an architect, a background that some critics argue had more influence on his work than did European or Japanese avant-garde aesthetics. He cohabitated with the working mistress of a "coffee shop" that he owned, contracted tuberculosis and, shortly after his release from a Japanese prison in which he had been incarcerated for "thought crimes," died in Tokyo at the age of twenty-seven. Legend has it that his last request was for a lemon; his last breath filled with its scent.

He left behind a body of poetry, short fiction, and essays that still riddle and delight his readers. He is, hands down, the premier figure of the avant-garde in twentieth-century Korean letters, a fact attested to not only by disc jockeys, but by the massive volume of criticism his work has garnered both in Korea and abroad.

◆

Reading Hahm Dong-seon after reading Yi Sang is like donning one's workaday clothes after dancing all night at an Iggy Pop Halloween potluck, which is to say that we hope it will provide a sense of the variety alive in a culture and in a literature that we might be sometimes too quick to perceive as homogenous. Hahm Dong-seon's poems manage to be both colloquial and mellifluous, plangent and affirming. His language is exact and his expressions condensed. Intelligence and emotion are set in consort by way of images whose immediacy and accuracy bring to mind William Carlos Williams, whose gravity and quiet confidence we might associate with Elizabeth Bishop.

Indeed, we can find in Hahm Dong-seon's poems Williams' love of detail and place as well as Bishop's love of detail and sensitivity to exile. Sadly, Hahm Dong-seon's exile is not self-imposed. Born in Yonbaek in 1930, his home was, in fact, south of the 38th parallel. But in the fallout proceeding from the Korean War the powers-that-be saw fit to establish the DMZ with Yonbaek to the north. Hahm Dong-seon has not been allowed to return home since, nor has he had communication with any of his family there. He has, however, stood many times at the highest point of South Korea's Kanghwa Island from which he can see the roof of his childhood home.

Today Hahm Dong-seon lives and writes in Seoul, South Korea.

♦

Choi Young-mi, as you might have guessed, is another matter altogether. Combine the irreverence of Yi Sang with the emotive force of Hahm Dong-seon and add the fire of protest, the sensuality of illicit love, and the stubborn determination to be both a woman and a free individual, and you will begin to garner a feeling for the concerns of Choi Young-mi's uncompromising poems.

One of the most popular poets in South Korea today, Choi's poems spring from the sometimes not so polite details of her public and private life. And yet, it seems odd to refer to her as "confessional" given that word's connotations of utterance born out of guilt, of revelation that hopes to leave its confessor shriven of her transgressions. Choi Young-mi's poems may seem almost shy at times, but apologetic they are not.

Born in 1961 to a Catholic family living in an outlying area of Seoul, she attended college and was one of many students to participate in the often violently-suppressed pro-democracy riots of the 1980's, a decade that witnessed Korea's rapid economic growth alongside its new status as one of the world's largest importers of tear gas. Choi Young-mi was one of a secretive group of translators who dared to translate Karl Marx's *Capital;* this translation was published under a single pseudonym in 1987 and led to the arrest of the president of Yiron Kwa Silcheon Books.

Choi Young-mi's popularity has continued to rise since Changbi, Korea's leading literary publisher, issued her first volume of poems in 1994, *At Thirty, the Party Was Over,* a volume that went on to sell over a half-million copies.

◆

Despite a growing interest in Korean poetry in the past decade, translations from the Korean are still largely absent from the shelves of most bookstores where one might normally find at least a few volumes from the Chinese and Japanese. Our former Poet Laureate, Robert Hass, noted recently that "Modern Korean poetry, like the poetry of Eastern Europe, is inextricably entangled with the country's history in the twentieth century," a history for which the United States is at least partly responsible and of which we are largely unaware (*The Washington Post,* Jan. 4, 1998). While we do not pretend to offer anything here resembling a full survey of Korean poetry or its historical context in the past one hundred years, we do hope to bring at least a bit of its energy, variety, and relevance home to American readers, whether within or beyond the purview of academic programs in Asian or Korean Studies. Rather than selecting poets around a central "Korean" theme or literary moment, we have chosen three poets from three different generations with the aim of presenting a sense of the vision inherent in each of these poets, a sense of integrity and voice that might defy, however briefly, our efforts toward literary taxonomy.

Whether one takes Robert Frost's statement that poetry is what is lost in translation as a literal proclamation in the face of a real impossibility (a statement often taken out of context and tempered somewhat by the fact that Frost had been working on his own translations), we can perhaps all agree that a poem loses something in the process of translation. Given this inevitability, the translator's obligation is to assure that the poem at least gains something new as well, an obligation made more difficult to fulfill when the original language and the target language share very little, if anything, in terms of genealogy—as is the case when we move from Korean (with roots in the Altaic languages) to English (a member of the Indo-European language family).

This is all just to say that increased complexity brings with it an increased obligation for aesthetic integrity; what we have lost here in literal or informational accuracy, we hope to compensate by fidelity to tone, to the sense and the personality of the original poem. Walter Benjamin argues that translation as mere conveyance of information is "the hallmark of bad translations." It has been our task as translators, our privilege and our pleasure, to help reincarnate these poems. A life and an afterlife, as Benjamin would have it. A spirit caught in the moment of transmigration, one body to another.

—James Kimbrell

THREE POETS OF MODERN KOREA

♦

Yi Sang

was trained as an architect during the period of Japanese occupation of the Korean peninsula. He was a controversial poet in his own time, and continues to provoke readers to this day. Incorporating a range of tone from the surreal to the hermetic, from the comic to the scientific, he is perhaps best known for his subversive blending of these sources with a more native Korean idiom. He was the author of numerous short stories and poems collected in various posthumous volumes. Arrested in Tokyo for "thought crimes" in 1937, he died in Japan of tuberculosis shortly after his release.

I Wed a Toy Bride

1. Night

The toy bride's skin smells like milk from time to time. Perhaps she'll give birth sooner or later. I put out the candle and whisper a scolding in the ear of the toy bride like this:

[Thou are like a newborn baby] . . .

The toy bride answers, sulking in the middle of the darkness.

[I have taken a walk to a pasture.]

The toy bride might come back, remembering the rich landscape of noon. She is warm like the notepad in my bosom. The scent of her is all that comes close to me. I waste away.

2. Night

If I give a needle to the toy bride, she will pierce some random object thoughtlessly. Calendar, book of poems, pocket-watch. And the place in my body where the past perches most closely.

This is proof that thorns rise in the mind of the toy bride. That is, like a rose...

My light body bleeds a little. I eat a fresh mandarin orange to cure the scar in the darkness whenever night comes.

The toy bride, who has only a ring in her body, looks for me, furling the dark like a curtain.

I am found out soon. Pain strikes me down—I thought the ring that touched my skin was a needle.

Lighting a candle, the toy bride looks for her mandarin orange.

I pretend to know nothing, and complain of no pain whatsoever.

Crow's-Eye View

Poem No. I

13 children rush down a street.
(A dead-end alley will suffice.)

The 1st child says it is terrifying.
The 2nd child also says it is terrifying.
The 3rd child also says it is terrifying.
The 4th child also says it is terrifying.
The 5th child also says it is terrifying.
The 6th child also says it is terrifying.
The 7th child also says it is terrifying.
The 8th child also says it is terrifying.
The 9th child also says it is terrifying.
The 10th child also says it is terrifying.

The 11th child says it is terrifying.
The 12th child also says it is terrifying.
The 13th child also says it is terrifying.
13 children have come together and are terrifying or terrified.
(The absence of any other condition would have been preferred.)

If one child amongst them is a terrifying child it's all right.

If two children amongst them are terrifying children it's all right.

If two children amongst them are terrified children it's all right.

If one child amongst them is a terrified child it's all right.

(An open alley will suffice.)

Though 13 children do not rush down the street everything is all right.

Poem No. II

    when my father dozes off beside me I become my father and I become my father's father though as ever my father just as he is is my father so why must I become my father's father's father's ... father *ad infinitum* why do I hurdle over my own father when I become my father and why at the last moment must I breathe life into my and my father's and my father's father's and my father's father's father's characters all at once

Poem No. III

the person fighting is namely the person who was not fighting
and the person who is fighting is also the one who does not fight and
if the case should arise that the person who is fighting wants to
watch some fighting it hardly matters if the person not fighting
watches the fighting or if the person that does not fight watches the
fighting or if the person who wasn't fighting or the person who does
not fight watches the absence of fighting

Poem No. IV

The problem regarding the patient's disposition

```
· 0987654321
0 · 987654321
09 · 87654321
098 · 7654321
0987 · 654321
09876 · 54321
098765 · 4321
0987654 · 321
09876543 · 21
098765432 · 1
0987654321 ·
```

Diagnosis 0:1

    26.10.1931

       The above diagnosis by the doctor in charge   Yi   Sang

Poem No. V

With regard to the inimitable traces after before-and-after and left-and-right were extracted

Though having giant wings I cannot fly   My sight is harbored in a narrow field

At the feet of the plump and dwarfish god I have fallen and have suffered a wound

Can a man with five viscera and six entrails be distinguished from an underwater cattle shed?

Poem No. VI

Parakeets　　*　Two parakeets

　　　　　　　　Two parakeets

　　　　　　*　Parakeets belong to the class Mammalia.

What I know of these two is that I do not know them. I have not, however, given up hope.

Parakeets　　Two parakeets

"Is this young woman the wife of the gentlemen, Yi Sang?" "That is true."

I stood and watched the parakeets' fury. My face must have gone red with shame.

Parakeets　　Two parakeets

　　　　　　Two parakeets

Of course, I was exiled. Or rather not so much exiled—I left voluntarily and was never banished. My body had so lost its central axis that it was heading off in every direction, and so I sobbed my minor tears.

"This is the very place." "I." "My—self—you and me."

"I."

What is the sCANDAL? "You...." "It's you."

"It's you, right?" "It's you." "No, it's definitely you."

Soaking wet, I ran off like a beast. Of course, even though there was no one who knew of this, no one who saw, I wonder if it was true, or if any of it ever happened at all.

Poem No. VII

branch of a tree in a land of endless exile · flowers blooming on a
branch · a peculiar tree that blooms in April · thirty wheels · a clear
mirror beside each wheel · a full moon's bitter descent toward a
horizon blithe as a sprout · in the energy of the mountain valley's
pure water, a full moon scraped up and dizzy with its nose cut off for
punishment · a letter from home that enters and wanders through a
land of exile · i lived barely sheltered from the cold · hazy sprout of
moon · colossal distance of an atmosphere in its own abiding silence
· a cavern crowded with nothing in which I spent a year and four
months in a state of fatigue and destitution · a constellation that
limps and falls down, gargantuan time that runs away and cuts the
alley into tiny stars · a sandstorm descending · pulverized rock salt
stained blood-red · my brain regarded as a lightening rod my bones
splendor soaked · i was locked underground like a venomous snake
in its high tower and could not move my limbs again · until the
sparkling heavens come

Poem No. VIII: Anatomy

Exam: the first part

operation table	1
plane mirror (mercury applied to back of glass)	1
air pressure	twice mean air pressure
temperature	none

First, holding the front side of an anesthetized three-dimensional subject up to the reflection of the whole in the plane mirror. In the plane mirror, transferring the application of mercury to the side opposite the present side. (With care not to let the light slip in) gradually neutralizing the anesthesia. Providing a pen and a piece of white paper. (The examiner absolutely avoiding the embrace of the examinee.) Releasing the examinee from the operation room, accordingly. The next day. Cutting the plane mirror in half, penetrating its vertical axis. Mercury twice applied.

Etc.... Not having yet acquired the satisfactory anatomical result.

Exam: the second part

    upright plane mirror   1

    assistant   several

    Choosing the vacuum of open air. First, attaching the hand-ends of two anesthetized arms to the surface of the mirror. Peeling mercury from the plane mirror. Removing the plane mirror. (Meanwhile, temporarily returning the mirror so that the reflection of the two arms is certain to remain.) Up to the shoulder-end of the two arms. Then, applying mercury (on the mirror's existing surface). At this time, taking away the vacuum from the revolution and rotation of the earth. Until taking in the two pairs of arms without exception. The next day. Bringing the glass forward. Again, applying a mercurial column on the existing surface. (Disposal of the two arms) (or reduction of the two arms) and continue. Repetition of switching the side on which mercury was applied and of the mirror's removal and continue.

    Etc.... Future steps not being known.

Poem No. IX: Gun Barrel

Everyday a hot wind blows in and, at last, a large hand reaches around my waist. As soon as the smell of my sweat has filled the ravines of the hand's fingertips—shoot! I will shoot! I feel the weight of a gun barrel in my stomach, the muzzle sliding up against the back of my teeth. When I closed my eyes as if ready for the rifle's blast, what was it that I spit out instead of a bullet?

Poem No. X: Butterfly

A shred of torn wallpaper calls a dying butterfly to mind. It is a secret mouth in touch with the other world. One day, I see a dying butterfly, examining my beard in the mirror. The butterfly with drooping wings drinks dewdrops curdled in a warm breath. If I die pressing my hand over my mouth, the butterfly will fly away as if to stand up just after my sitting down. I'll keep this secret inside.

Poem No. XI

    This porcelain cup looks like my skull. When I take the cup in hand, an arm like a grafted branch sprouts from my arm and the hand that hangs from the upstart arm snatches the porcelain cup and flings it over my shoulder to the floor. Because my arm defends the porcelain cup to the death, the broken bits of cup are, of course, my own skull that looks like the porcelain cup. Even if my arm had so much as flinched before the branching arm twisted snakelike back into my arm, the white paper holding off the flood would have been ripped. But as expected my arm defends the porcelain cup to the final breath.

Poem No. XII

A loose bundle of dirty clothes flies up into the air and drops. It is a flock of white doves. It is a bit of propaganda that on the other side of this sky as small as my palm, the war has ended and peace has arrived. One flock of doves gleans the dirt from its feathers. On this side of the sky small as my palm, the war begins, the dirty war that pummels the white doves with a wooden club. If the air turns thick with soot, the flock of white doves veers off again to the other side of the sky no larger than my palm.

Poem No. XIII

My arms were severed and fell to the ground, still holding the razor. If I examine them closely, they appear to have gone pale as if horrified by something. Thus, I converted these arms into candleholders and set them up in my room for decoration. Even after their lives leave them, the arms are afraid of me, perhaps more than ever. I regard my own slight manner more highly than a flowerpot.

Poem No. XIV

There is a grassy field in front of an ancient castle where I sat, took off my hat and laid it on the ground. I tied a heavy stone to all that I remembered and hurled it from the turret. The dolorous sound of history moving in reverse along the parabola. That's when I looked down from the castle and saw a beggar standing like a totem pole next to my hat. Despite appearances to the contrary, the beggar on the ground is high above me. Or perhaps he is the long departed ghost of history *in toto*? The darkness inside the hollow of the hat hails the imminent sky. Without warning, the beggar bends forward, shaking with fear, and thrusts a stone into my hat. I had already fainted. A vision of a map on which my heart is seen migrating into my skull. A cold hand touches my forehead. The hand left a mark on my skin that never was erased.

Poem No. XV

1

I am in the main room, which has no mirror. The *I* which I left in the mirror is also absent. Now, I am shaking for fear of my *I* in the mirror. I wonder whether the *I* in the mirror is weaving a plot to hurt me while he is somewhere else.

2

I slept on a cold bed bearing a crime. I was absent from my dream. Military boots filled with false legs dirtied my dream's white paper.

3

I secretly enter a room where a mirror is hanging that I might release myself from the mirror. But my *I* in the mirror enters as well with a gloomy face. The *I* in the mirror expresses his regret at me. Just as I am behind bars because of him, he is trembling, imprisoned by me.

4

My dream where I am not. My mirror where my imposter does not show up. He who longs for my solitude—there's no problem, even if solitude is merely idle. At last, I decided to recommend suicide for my *I* in the mirror. I pointed him toward a small window in the upper corner of the room, a window without a view. The window was tailored especially for suicide. My *I* in the mirror had a point: if I don't kill myself as well, he will be incapable of leaving. My *I* in the mirror is close to the phoenix.

5

I covered my heart with a bulletproof metal and fired the pistol, aiming at the left side of the mirror. The bullet dug into the left of his chest but his heart was on the right.

6

Red ink spilled from the dummy heart. In my dream (the one I was late for), I was condemned to capital punishment. I did not control my dream. It is a serious crime that separates people who can't shake hands.

Distance

—a case in which a woman absconded—

Lines of a railroad laid out on white paper. This is the diagram of my mind cooling. Each day, I send a telegram in which untruths are written down: arrival tomorrow evening. Each day, I send my necessities by parcel post. My life is becoming better acquainted with this distance that resembles nothing so much as a disaster area.

Hahm Dong-seon

was born in 1930 in Yonbaek, Hwanghae Province.
Though Yonbaek was located in the South when
Korea was partitioned after World War Two, it
became a part of North Korea after the cease-fire of
the Korean War in 1953. Exiled from his home,
Hahm Dong-seon has acted as Chairman of the
Korean Modern Poets Association, and as Vice
Chairman and past-President of Korean PEN. An
established poet, literary commentator, and essay-
ist, Hahm Dong-seon is the author of many books
including *Short Time, Long Story* (Seoul: Sanmok,
1997), *Thinking of Home from a Distance* (Seoul:
Kyongwon Publishers, 1994) and *Colony* (Seoul:
Chunghanmunhwa Sa, 1986). He is Professor
Emeritus at Chung Ang University in Seoul.

Record of a Journey

If I go to my old home,

If I go to my old home on this journey,

I will see the doorway where we once stood

Gauging our height with a notched string

Gone slack by now like an old clothesline

    anchored to a pole.

And in this train that rattles with speed

I watch the wind-pulled stalks of corn

Lean their weight toward the passenger cars

That stir the same insects I fanned away

    when I was a child —

But now I am going to Pusan.

Sweat blears the lines I drew in my palm

As if to map the footpaths between the checkered

    paddies back home,

And Old Wart's lookout,

Where nightly we crept away with melons,

Disappears without notice.

The brackish sunlight off the ocean

Comes toward me as if across a stretch of shattered glass

And stings my eyes to a watery red.

The sky is streaked with a sudden summer shower,

And my face is stitched in the haze of the wide
    carriage window;
My mother's face rises up in mine
And from her face the quick rain streams down.

Park Su-keun

—*after Park Su-keun's* A Tree and Two Women, *oil on canvas, 1962*

There's a leafless tree between the woman with the baby
    tied to her back
And the woman holding a bamboo basket on her head.
Hair arranged in a coiled knot,
White jacket and black skirt,
Worn-out wadded baby blanket,
Black rubber shoes
Have gone nowhere in the painting
The surface of which calls to mind the touch of granite
    or a rust-colored road.
At what point in the war
Could this have been the place where we were living?
That was forty years ago, another spring is coming on.
The road he walked
Cuts through winter, the wind still cold all day.

Full Moon

As legend would have it, the nettle's branches slant toward wind

And its fruit surrounds the tutelary shrine.

My mother wearing white so white that it rubs out the darkness

Makes her way to the shrine

Carrying the ripe moon like a water jar on top of her head.

Each time she prays she spills water and her prayers wash over

     every crag and nook of this land

Possessed by evil spirits.

Still, her youngest son who fled from the war has not yet been seen.

The wormwood grows head-high and taller,

And ever since a voice spoke through the shaman and said

     This is all your fault!

Beneath each full moon

My mother lights a candle.

A Rough Sketch of Autumn

Shadows of the bluish-black pine forest

Harbor the trestle, the field of eulalia

And graze along the first footholds of the mountain.

A dragonfly threading the curved creek bank

Seems stunned by the shadows

And lights on a cosmos

That blooms in a tilt as though counting on the wind

    to come back soon.

At the gates of the village

The long sound of autumn comes in a quaver,

The throat notes of someone singing *pansori*.

Over a grandmother's stooped shoulders,

The sun in autumn, whether it wants to or not,

Disappears as soon as it nears the horizon.

In my heart

A parched leaf is always sculling past.

Colony

How terribly compulsion and oppression

Made us stand in every cranny and corner!

On the precipice, on the edge of the precipice, below the precipice,

On every side, we were terrified of making a sound.

Our house was

Like so many sea-plant scraps

Washed in by waves

And shoved against the rocks.

And then one day violence made us sit in one spot

And another day told us to stand up

Like cows loaded with packsaddles.

And when violence covered us from head to toe

A cuckoo's song,

Low but clear

Came in from the stream's far side.

With the cuckoo's note, evenings came and went and so did
     the summers,

And in those days when time was picked away bit by bit,

My older brother

Whose blood was hot for independence

Was carted off to jail.

All night long, a katydid reeled out its sorrow in the bush.

As spiritless as stagnant water, my whole family

Trembled like skinny poplars

That bend for even the weakest breeze,

But my father still clenched his teeth each time after saying,

"Those people pretend to win because we pretend to lose,"

And he died from a bottlenecked rage

Before he saw the sovereignty he wished for even in sleep.

After that, like huge dragonflies darting about,

B-29 bombers shocked us

As if we'd heard tin foil

Rattled in a witch's hands.

When everything was done,

A quiet peace

Like cool moisture spreading across paper windows

    and doors

Was the first and last pleasure under colonial reign.

My delight in that moment slipped through my hands,

But it is as clear today as it ever was,

This memory of

My body and mind swelling

Tight as a bowstring.

Autumn Sanjo

The cosmos are out along the field-paths.

The noon light that falls on the petals in October

Clears its throat when the clouds pass over.

Flying in from who knows where a worn out honeybee

That could likely not buzz another ten *li*

Sinks inside the petals as if it had journeyed all that way

    just to collapse there.

Its breath is like moonlight on a knife-blade.

Wind weathers the leaves of the grapevine;

The season is restless, ready to follow

The crowd of wind-scattered petals

That fall like the tears of a woman who met her desire

    late one autumn

And confessed that love.

Island

After setting out toward the east this morning
I return to the gloam of the western sea.
Beneath the first stars the boat lights come on
One by one like a woman's most constant regrets.
The village behind the stonewall and tree line
Looms up with one step, draws back with another.
Will the unmistakable smell of bean-paste stew
That has haunted this road's entrance for years
Be the last thing I take into account today?
Memories are ephemeral, hard to see.
Soon they're the same as the summer that poisons
    the oleanders,
The slow-breaking branches of lust.

Thought in Several Pieces

My love moves forward
With all the day's undulations,
And falls headlong
Into an overturned century,
And my love remains
To this day
Like a speck that cannot be wiped away
From a freshly spread tablecloth.
I walk down the street that swelters
Like a gourd in July gone tough and stringy,
And the flower tree that I stop by each day,
Its roots branching out in my chest,
Says that I might happen to meet her
On the path along the back wall of Doksu Palace,
On a tree-lined avenue in Dongsung Dong,
Or, perhaps, on a bench in the park.
Passing by Kwangwha Gate,
Among rivers of people
That crowd together like tadpoles in a drought's last
    water puddle,
After passing Jongno and Hwashin where the coffee
    stains my fingers,

I arrive in Mukyo Dong

And the newsboy's papers folded in layers beneath his arm

Remind me of your long hair

And I hear you saying as you used to say

That rainbows only form after weeping;

I open the paper

And, of course, you are not there,

Though a new story on the Korean War

Has caught my eye.

Journal in Jumunjin

As if painted with a thick brush, the horizon
Goes down to dusk
And night begins to settle in the empty shoreline fields.
My hometown, like the stars just blinking on,
Is somewhere on the other side of a wide, wide river —
More sensation, more memory than town.
The raw-fish restaurant sways
With the dizzy give and take of the ocean waves.
The lights from docked fishing boats are doubled
In my cup of rice wine —
I drink and drink
And though I will soon quit this work, I haven't yet
	looked enough
Through the train window at the trees and fields slipping
	out of eyeshot.
A handful of wind rises
Hauled away by night's dark skirt.

Landscape

After the rain

Fell hard on the autumn roofs,

From the most far-flung house to the nearest village

You can hear the ripe persimmons

Heavy with the sun's red setting

Muttering now amongst themselves

That they are on the verge of falling.

As soon as the sun went under

As if hiccupped by the horizon,

The wind pulled in behind a train arriving from the surburbs

And let the night swell across

The field that turns

An annual crop, more or less, for fifty homes.

Before long electric bulbs are hot with light

And the first night of frost goes warm

Like the spot on the floor above the heat

    piped in from the kitchen fire,

A crescent moon pokes out its face

Like the curved back of a long-toothed comb.

In the Season of Ripened Barley...

In the season of ripened barley the cuckoo's notes
Waver like my uncle's sighs broken up
By the clanking of the train to Bukgan-do.
The cuckoo sheds its notes like my mother sheds tears.
When the wind blows all at once across the barley
The month of my birth
The month of May in the lunar pages
Makes a sound like crumpling foil
And is nearer now than ever before.
Perhaps this stems from my ancestors' unrequited wishes
Which have taken the color of the tough plantain flowers
Along the banks of the reservoir skirted by poplars.
Now those wishes cast an eye hot as the iron wheels of a cart
Driven across a field of stones.

In Tunnel Number Three

Feigning an effort to stop the war, the big powers took our side,

Then ran off the owners and settled down in our living rooms.

Now their legacy composes that great work of history

In the demilitarized zone around the armistice line.

The tunnel—south-north, high-low—opens

Where the gunfire that ached in our ears metamorphosed

    the mountains to rubble,

Where the knife's blade made the river water boil and horrified

    each one watching.

We've all heard that silence creates its own terror—

With each step forward

The far end of the tunnel becomes one black brush-stroke

Except for the back of my brother who was taken north

From the public hall

And bound like a string of dried croaker.

A quick light off his shoulders flickers sometimes in the drops

    that fall from the roof of the tunnel.

When I crawled out of that hole, forty years

Of refracted unease stood directly in front of me.

Sunlight slips off the tips of my fingers,

And on the hill that I keep sinking into

The daisy fleabane—the one that I saw

In the days of war when I traveled back and forth from this

    to the other world—

The daisy fleabane blooms

Like the sound of the hand bell in a funeral procession.

Mara Island

Gromwells and orchids dot the field

With a mulberry color like the lips of women

    sea-plant divers.

The land here is level as an old floor cushion.

If I open my hands while I'm sitting here, the whole

    scene is filled in with me

Wondering if this island is the beginning or the end

    of our country.

A stone loosened

By the rocking ocean

Falls into Moseul Port

And the wind stirs up

A day-long night-long world of grief in my mind.

After the last trace of dusk,

The fist-sized stars that guide the ships

Ease down and rest on Virgin Rock

Where the goats used to chew their cuds.

The chugging of engines and the voices of men

    heading offshore on the fishing boats

Won't let me sleep tonight.

And so I have come through the woods on this path

    filled with butterflies.

Propped up on a rock as big as a house,
Night lifts the island up toward the East.

The Last Face

Close to dawn, the moonlight

That made my teeth cold

Shone between the thatched straws of the water mill.

After my mother sewed a charm

In the waistline of my pants, the pants of her youngest son,

The one about to take leave of the war,

She described in detail the landmarks that I might

    need to escape,

She pointed them out as if I were looking at an un-

    folded map.

I ran about fifteen *li* in one long stretch

Alongside the mountain, the stream and field,

And arrived, breathless, at the ferry crossing.

Past the mountain, past the field, I saw

The moon   how it must have floated in the stream

    long before I got there.

By the time I became a full-grown man,

That charm was

Worn to a knot of sweat-soaked threads,

But I can still see my mother's face in the frayed edges.

If I pick up her face, if I hold her face,

The moon will ask me how I am doing,

The moon will wave its white hand.

Fisherman's Morning

When morning first steps down through the darkness

And the hour is already muggy with dew,

In this fishing village entire years

Gather and stand inches apart.

When the sky is no larger than a bean,

Than an aperture in the instant after the picture,

With a great motion

The fishermen are led by fishing nets.

It may be true that summer has a skin slick

As low-tide seawater,

But what better now than a cigarette

While it dawns on me that each fisherman's stride

Is the single fact,

Is the beginning and the end

Of this life and this work.

Jeju Island

—Sajebi Hill

Traveling over the long ages

And never forgetting how thick old Chusa's hair grew

    in his island prison,

The grandmother of the mountain was turned into a tree

    bound in a pot.

When the dark that draws around the island's peaks and slopes

Is stepped into, when it gives off the muffled crunch of snow

    underfoot,

The island can not drift toward sleep, not with all that noise

And the work of oars rowing in another banished man,

And the racket of prisoners turning pages in their books.

The place of exile

Floats freely in water,

Wind at the helm.

Choi Young-mi

was born in 1961. She received her B.A. in Western Art History from Seoul National University and an M.A. in Art History from Hong-ik University. When the Democratization Struggle of 1980 turned to a bloody massacre in Kwanju, South Korea, and hundreds—if not thousands—of demonstrators were killed, Choi Young-mi became active in the student pro-democracy struggle. Though scorned by some critics for her candid depiction of political realities and personal, often sexual, relationships, her first volume of poems, *At Thirty the Party Was Over* (1994) has sold over half a million copies. She is the author of a second volume of poems, *Bicycling in Dreamland* (Seoul: Changbi, 1998) as well as a collection of travel writing, *Melancholy of the Era* (Seoul: Changbi, 1997). She is currently at work on her first novel.

A Page from My Childhood Journal

When I saw the sun turn blood-red for the first time, I thought
a fire was spreading through the sky. I ran to my mother in tears.
"Mom," I cried, "the sky is on fire!" How sour was her bosom!

Why is the sunset red?
Deluxe cars lining the curb before a shabby whorehouse.
A woman who does not age, a man who does not sleep.
A wardrobe door always half-open.
A television left on and no one watching.
A child blowing bubbles all day.

With so much of that evening
left unexplained, the wall of my childhood offered no passage.

At Thirty, the Party Was Over

Of course, I know
I liked the demonstrators more than the demonstrations,
and the feel of the barroom more than the booze,
and that when I was lonely, I enjoyed love songs in a low voice
more than all the combative ditties that began with "Comrades!"
And this makes no difference at all...

The party was over.
Drinks ran out, people poked their wallets back into their pockets,
and my love, too, finally walked out
while the rest of them tallied the last calculation
and left after finding their shoes...
But I know
that someone will stay here until it's all over, and clean the table
before the owner comes out, and work up a batch of hot tears
remembering all that happened,
and someone will sing changes into the song he left unfinished.
Perhaps, perhaps
someone will prepare a table instead of him

and gather everyone up again.

Lights will be turned back on—the stage will be readied.

And this makes no difference at all....

In Sokcho

I was seven years old when I learned that waves were the ocean rocking.

Landscapes from long ago rise and make a chain of islands. Once or twice when I kicked up the sand, things I'd forgotten turned up again, and the day passed and I hardly noticed, and the seagulls moved their shoulders up and down like frivolous rumors. Once, where the ocean marked the dry sand, my lover left, and the waves repeated themselves, and the foam said it all again. Oh, my head was bedridden, swimming with waiting for the next wave. In the first moment of waking, clouds came in herds and the sound of the waves got caught in the hair over my ears and echoed like bombs exploding.

I was thirty-two years old when I learned that pushing while being pushed was waves.

Whatever will fall has fallen, but the rain keeps on. Regardless of where I lie down, a rainy night shows up dragging in its fish-smell like an old curtain. It's late now, and the rain stirs up the stink of fish that I can't wash my hands of, and names I knew go under with a splash down by the shoreline. My pride droops like squids hung out to dry on the clothesline, and the tide won't rise again, and time won't, no matter what I think. Still, when I look at the aquarium in the window at the raw-fish restaurant, my button-shaped eyes like the eyes of a breathing squid, oh, then death races up with bright lights flashing. Before you lean toward me, I will lean toward you.

For T———, Light Red over Black

Now a photograph of some other woman
with breasts like melons grins on the far wall of your room.

Now another pretty face lies down in your dream's
        territory
and sleeps with her head in the crook of your arm.

One day anonymous flowers blossomed
in the grasslands of my youth's sweetest oblivion.

When I turn my memory's random, dogeared pages
sun blears the landscape's yellowed margins.

Take the painting the color of dark blood
out of its frame.

I'll come to you
in those blunt drops.

Trees

Trees are everywhere.

There are poplars that divide the sidewalks from roads like a barbed-
   wire fence;

trees are floating, shimmering

in your eyes still clouded with sleep on your way to the office,

and there are trees in the book of poetry that dozes in the display
   table,

and trees in the street cleaner's solitary glass of *soju*.

At dawn when my mother bears the cross of her life with her rosary
   in hand,

and in the broad chest of my lover,

and between this and the next world,

trees are taking their stand.

Or there are no trees.

Neither at Seoul Grand Park's botanical garden,

nor at the grade school's first-day ceremonies, nor on the television's
   weekend movie,

are trees seen at all.

Even in Schubert's *Winter Journey,*

even on the most faded, yellow museum canvas,

even from the bus window on the way to Seonun Temple,

and ... ah, even at my bedside —

there were no trees under which I could lie with comfort.

In a Subway, # 4

Three women are dozing off,
a woman's head leaning against a woman's shoulder,
the woman's shoulder over a woman's chest,
the woman's tiredness on another's worries,
do, re, mi, side by side.

Three men are boarding,
boring their way through the passengers' sluggish
    parboiled gazes;
three men step into the swell of subway flesh
packed tight as if wrapped in pork skin.

First, a beggar holds out his hand.
Next, a blind man sings a song.
After them,
a bushy-headed prophet shouts everyone awake,
"Brothers and Sisters, prepare for the end!"
Three women are dozing off.
Three men are fast approaching.

Eleven o'clock in the morning,
The subway is full of the unemployed.

Some Reincarnation

I do not believe the proposition
that spirits come around in April
as buds, as flowers.

I do not believe the poem that claims
the shades that left the earth in May
weep dolefully, changed to wind.

I cannot believe the song
that says the young one (I was standing right there)
that fell on the rowdy street in June
has now assumed the form of a flower, or wind,
    or anything else.
I cannot even dream it.

Back from the dead, this morning opens its eyes
with minimum travel,
no need to roam like a flower, like wind.

When the desk lamp flickers on
a riot of voices rushes straight for me.

The Mind's Mediterranean

On the shore where the dandruff-colored seagulls
make me dizzy,

The wind doesn't blow,
and the waves hardly come in.

The Mediterranean is a pond in my mind.
It holds its own blemished body.
Its water twitches.

Locked away in the jail of all this pining,
the waters can't begin to budge toward shore —
no wind or rain will raise them.

I'm waiting for the perfection of silence.

Like the noon sun that departs
after warming my forehead,
like the fog that clears quickly
after its slow rising,

Did you think I'd walk off

without so much as a hint?

Song in a Dolorous Café

It seems as though I've stopped here before,
seems I drank here one day
in this light, this seat, this café.
The madam with slightly sunken dimples,
her eyes, her smile looks far too familiar.

With which chap
did I pluck the flower of random desire
    without any guilt at all?
With which one did I find some excuse for a little bit of darkness?
Was it when my blood peaked at scalding
that I scratched and licked the whole night long
feigning some random ill
or concocting an itch, an artificial swelling?

We pillaged each bar-wretch and -wench.
We hacked away at their sob stories
on the chopping board of inebriated pity.
We laughed, we beat our fists on the table,
we guzzled our drinks and sang,
and once or twice our vision got tangled.
So well...

Fear is mine and shame on me.

This seat, this café, the witness of my debauchery.

Amen 1

+

++

+++

++++

Lord, have pity on us.

Ambassadors of fire assumed their posts in the sky above Seoul
and commenced praying.

Rivalry of electric crosses, some higher, some lower,
antennas of the meek, necks to the ground,
heaven is a long way off—
oh diligent electric tubes that decorate
the tacky nights of the *fin de siècle,*
how long can you keep flickering, bleary-eyed from dreaming
    of the impossibly remote?

Over the tomb of desire, red and rising,
The bloodshot eyes of the insomniac city issue the following:
Those who suffer, those who undertake a burden, all of you, come to me.
I will let you rest in peace.

Amen.

No little star appears with an answer, and my heart (hanging
from the hazy air),

my heart (a nail hammered through it) waits for the word.

It was a holy, holy night.

Amen 2

++++
+++
++
+

After the crusaders withdrew their guards from the dead city,

A stray dog, skittish beneath the unplugged sky, beneath the night
    gone darker than night,

Lowers his tail and sniffs around the park.

And it rains.

On a vacant bench in an apartment playground,
on the creased eyelids of a sleepless night,
on the switched-off neon signs of God,
on the public graveyard of monumental desires,
the steaming rain falls.
An unrelieved soul stands up in a hurry to eat
And jerks open the refrigerator door:
stone-cold food of the earth.

The judgment day is nowhere near —
when will peace dwell in this sour sleepwalking stomach?

It was a silent, silent night.

Birds, Even Now...

Between one asphalt road and another,
high in the wind-stripped winter branches,
you build in breakneck spells of construction.

Never mind the soot, the northeastern wind,
you shape a kingdom that will not flinch
amid the roaring cranes, the playground noises.
Your quarters go up in twig-black patches
darker than the skyward grime of Seoul.

All for the sake of next spring's hatchlings,
your wings beat now in a flurry of labor.
After the heavy sleep of darkness,
after the first inch of daybreak,
the twigs of Mt. Bukhan fit tight in your beak.

Faithful as ever to the world of seen things
     long since seen,
to all the myriad anchors of desire,
you do not take leave from the human city.
Even now
your houses are multiplying.

While I lounged in my blankets, scratching my nose,
while people were all in a stir at breakfast
    by the news of the fall of the Soviet Union,
branch by branch your walls were erected,
without rumor, without sound.

Each nest with its own colossal architecture
swells to a sphere with the ticking of seconds.

No sooner than the first sweet sting of March wind
the little birds will kick clear of their shells.

Do birds build their round houses so quietly
in Moscow?

My heart it seems is a nest of shame,
and even today you are building your homes.

And...

There are days when I am completely useless.

The uncorked bottle of wine might sway its weight in the refrigerator,

but there are days when I can neither drink nor smoke.

One by one numbers are erased, fraying the pages of my little black

    book.

Ready to meet a new man, a woman wearing the scarf given to her

by an old lover stands looking into a mirror.

Snot is drying along the corner of a half-read newspaper.

Time rises up clearly in autumnal sunlight,

time swells like a tomb

in the day with which I must find something to do.

Recollection of the Last Sex

At breakfast, picking dried croaker off of its bones,

I saw the secret of the body

finally laid bare:

Tangle of disconnected organs, spots of flesh.

Is the truth like this?

Stripped of skin, the meat and bones of it remain,

And the story becomes quite simple, reticence of our secret bodies

    on that last night.

Picking dried fish off its bones, I think that

Scars are the clothes a living person puts on.

I promised to stay unblemished.

I had too much love like that;

quick as scales scraped off a fish, clouds of unknowing were lifted

    layer by layer,

and the sun's rays fell in a baroque multitude.

The light on our skin shrank us.

I don't know who got up first, but we threw our clothes on as quick

    as cold scales

will stick to a body.

After loosing the pulse of conversation,

after all the bodily wanting,

I chewed for a long time

on the recollection of the last sex

that filled my mouth.

Dead Leaf and Child

Somewhere
a leaf is shaking on its branch.

A leaf is plucked by the wind and falls
that it might shine and be taken as a cold metaphor in the midst
    of someone's excavation,
that it might announce the secrets of the great sun and earth,
that it might be exhibited as the open remains of the season.

Somewhere a leaf is pulled by the wind and descends
to the ground after much resistance,
and somewhere is a child who stops crying long enough
to pick up that sudden toy of nature.

Somewhere the tip-end of a dead leaf points to the sky,
to the reason things come and the reason things go
midway through the long last breath....

In the Submerged Area of Imha Dam

Without you, my mind will not fall under any landscape's spell,

but I see your face at the tip of a branch

in the drowned forest, in the skyward arms.

Meditations on an oblivion of summers,

everyone's truth in a stream of truth,

all the dust my life gave life to,

it's all knocking along the river now, falling apart as the sun goes,

pulled into time which no one can step away from,

    no one can swallow.

That October, leaves fell before losing their green and floated around

    like lame ships,

but I was all stillness on the river bluff.

Prisons that I built and wiped-out in one fell swoop of a life.

Antique sighs as yet unanswered.

I wish they would sink under their own weight.

That October, I sat on the river bluff and cast loose

what was left of a done-for youth. I let thirty-five years go.

Emptiness on both sides of my hand.

NOTES

♦

Yi Sang

"Crow's-Eye View" is a single word, created by Yi Sang by omitting one horizontal line from the Chinese pictograph meaning "bird." Fifteen sections of this poem were originally published in *Chosun Chungang Ilbo* from July 24–August 8, 1934. Eight other sections under the same title (written in Japanese) were published prior to this in *Chosun and Architecture* (1931). The sections that we have translated here constitute the whole of the "Crow's-Eye View" published in 1934.

"Distance" was originally written in Japanese and was published after the poet's death.

Hahm Dong-seon

"Park Su-keun." Park Su-keun (1914–1965) was a Korean painter who focused primarily on the emotional states of common people via stylized subject matter and the intense use of grayish- white and brown. The painting that the poet refers to here is *A Tree and Two Women,* oil on canvas (1962).

"A Rough Sketch of Autumn." *Pansori* is a traditional Korean folk music that gained its highest popularity in the late nineteenth century and became less common during Japan's occupation of Korea. In *pansori,* a performer sings a song of a narrative inflected by satire, humor, and / or parody punctuated by a single drummer.

"Autumn Sanjo." *Sanjo* is a solo played with traditional Korean instruments that was developed in southern Korea at the end of the nineteenth century. It has an impromptu form and usually begins with a slow rhythm and ends with a rapid rhythm and requires the accompaniment of an hourglass-shaped drum.

"Thought in Several Pieces." Located in Seoul, Doksu Palace was built during the Chosun Dynasty. Today, the path that runs behind the palace is well-maintained, and is a popular meeting place for young couples. Kwanghwa Gate is the main entrance of the Kyongbok Palace in Seoul. Dongsung Dong, Mukyo Dong, Jongno, and Hwashin are street names in Seoul.

"In the Season of Ripened Barley. . . ." *Bukgan-do* constitutes the majority of the land area known today as the Yanbian Korean Autonmous Prefecture, eastern Jilin Province, China, formerly a part of the Korean territory. The last of many border disputes between China and Korea took place in 1909, and resulted in Chinese victory and possession of this land due largely to diplomatic maneuvers on the part of the Japanese government. "Do" is the Korean suffix used to designate an island; though *Bukgan-do* is not a literal island, it is referred to as an island by the Korean people who view it as an island between two countries, Korea and China. Bukgan-do became a central location in the Korean resistance movement against colonial Japan.

"Autumn Sanjo," "The Last Face." *li* is a unit of distance occasionally used in Korea. 1 *li* is about 0.4 km.

"Jeju Island." Chusa is one of Kim Jung-heuy's pen names. Kim was a scholar, calligrapher, and epigraphist (1786–1856) in the late Chosun Dynasty. He was exiled in Jeju Island for nine years because of the political turmoil in 1840.

Choi Young-mi

"For T_____, Light Red over Black." This poem takes its title from Mark Rothko's *Light Red over Black*, oil on canvas (1957).

"Trees." *Soju* is a popular Korean liquor made from distilled grain.

"Some Reincarnation." April, May, and June in this poem allude to specific moments in the history of modern Korea. The April Revolution (April 19, 1960) was led by students and citizens eager to bring democracy to Korean society and resulted in over 6,000 casualties, President Lee Seung-mahn's resignation, and the collapse of the ruling Liberty Party. In May, 1980, the Kwangju Democratization Struggle took place in the city of Kwangju. Countless protesters were killed and wounded when the Korean Army began to fire indiscriminately. The June Democracy Struggle (June 10, 1987) was a nationwide movement against prolonged military rule; protesters demanded the right to elect their president directly. There were many casualties here as well. This protest, however, laid the foundation for a peaceful transfer of political regimes.

THE TRANSLATORS

Yu Jung-yul was born in Pusan, South Korea, in 1969. She holds degrees in French Literature from Pusan National University, and is a Phi Beta Kappa graduate of Kenyon College. A painter, freelance photographer and translator, she also holds an M.F.A. in Studio Art from Florida State University.

James Kimbrell was born in Jackson, Mississippi, in 1967. He is a graduate of Millsaps College, the University of Southern Mississippi, the University of Virginia, and the University of Missouri, Columbia. He is the author of a volume of poems, *The Gatehouse Heaven* (Sarabande, 1998), and is the recipient of a Ruth Lilly Fellowship, a "Discovery"/*The Nation* Award, *Poetry* magazine's Bess Hokin Award, and a Whiting Writers' Award. He teaches in the Creative Writing program at Florida State University.